101 WAYS TO ROMANCE
YOUR WIFE GOD'S WAY

Don,

May God richly bless you!

Charles R

101 WAYS TO ROMANCE
YOUR WIFE GOD'S WAY

Charles Roberts

Outskirts Press, Inc.
Denver, Colorado

101 Ways to Romance Your Wife God's Way
All Rights Reserved.
Copyright © 2011 Charles Roberts
v4.0 r1.0

Edited by Tiffany Hayes

All scripture quotations are taken from the *King James Version* of the Bible.

Cover Photo © 2011 JupiterImages Corporation. All rights reserved - used with permission.

Outskirts Press, Inc.
http://www.outskirtspress.com

ISBN: 978-1-4327-7818-7

Library of Congress Control Number: 2011912184

Outskirts Press and the "OP" logo are trademarks belonging to Outskirts Press, Inc.

PRINTED IN THE UNITED STATES OF AMERICA

Contents

Introduction

THE *BIBLE* SAYS, "God is not mocked, whatsoever a man sows, that shall he also reap (Galatians 6:7)". Men, do you find yourselves always frustrated because you are unable to connect with your wife like you used to? If so, it could be that you stopped sowing the seeds you once sowed while you were dating; seeds of tenderness, compassion, time, and resources.

Your wife is like a fertile field that requires constant cultivation. Sadly, many men stop courting their wives once the honeymoon is over. Some men feel like they no longer have to put forth the same effort they once did when they were pursuing their wives.

Marriage was ordained to be a reflection of God and His relationship with His people. The *Bible* refers to Christians as the bride of Christ. Christ is *always* in pursuit of His bride. He's always wooing her, telling her how much she means to Him. Men should be no different. One cannot plant apple seeds and expect to reap oranges; that would be crazy. So, why is it that most men expect to reap so much from their wives, yet spend very little time planting the seeds that will produce the desired harvest? The reasons may vary, but the good news is that help has arrived!

This book was written to assist every man who desires to rekindle the flames of passion and intimacy with his spouse. In this book, you will find new ways to make her smile. You will find out how doing the simplest things can make the biggest impact. In this book, you will find out that there are at least 101 ways to romance your wife God's way.

Whether she has communicated it to you or not, your wife longs for you to romance her. I challenge every man reading this book to apply at least one of these God inspired ideas once a week, and watch as your marriage goes to a whole new level. Be bold! Step out in faith by doing something you've never done before. Please, don't just make this a one-time event, but a change of lifestyle. Come on guys! Your wives are waiting.

101 Ways to Romance Your Wife God's Way

1) **When your wife gets home from a long day at work, ask her to relax on the couch while you take a warm towel and lay it on her eyes.**

Okay guys, we've all been there. After coming home after a long days work, the first question that we have for our wives is what are we having for dinner? Right? Wrong!

Instead of seeking to get your needs met, try ministering to your wife in this way, and I guarantee she'll appreciate your thoughtfulness.

And as you would that men should do to you, do ye also to them likewise. Luke 6:31

Results: _____

_____

_____

_____

_____

_____

_____

2)   When your wife arrives home after a long day, have a container of warm water ready so she can soak her feet. After she soaks her feet, you gently massage them.

Don't ever think you're too "macho" to minister to your wife. Miracles take place when you begin to minister. Consider the woman who washed Jesus' feet with her tears.

And, behold, a woman in the city, which was a sinner, when she knew that Jesus sat at meat in the Pharisee's house, brought an alabaster box of ointment, and stood at his feet behind him weeping, and began to wash his feet with tears, and did wipe them with the hairs of her head, and kissed his feet, and anointed them with the ointment. Luke 7:37-38

Results: _____

_____

_____

_____

_____

_____

_____

3)   Offer to lotion her back and feet.

There's nothing like a soft smooth body lying next to you, besides if she's going to put lotion on her body anyway, you might as well be the one to do it.

I have perfumed my bed with myrrh, aloes, and cinnamon. Proverbs 7:17

Results: _____

_____

_____

_____

_____

_____

_____

4)   Call your wife throughout the day. Let her know how much you miss her and how you appreciate all that she does.

We all like to know that we are appreciated, especially women. They have enough on their minds as it is, and being married to us may not be the easiest task in the world. Don't just rely on a greeting card to thank her; let her hear the words coming directly from your mouth.

A word fitly spoken is like apples of gold in pictures of silver. Proverbs 25:11

Results: _____

_____

_____

_____

_____

_____

_____

5)   Tell your wife how much she means to you, and tell her often.

How does it make you feel when you go to work every day and give your all, but no one ever takes the time to show their appreciation for your contribution to the company? Now, imagine how your wife must feel when you come home day after day and never tell her how much she means to you.

Or ministry let us wait on our ministering...Romans12:7

Results: _____

_____

_____

_____

_____

_____

_____

6) **Purchase a flower and break the stem really short. Before she leaves the house for work, place it behind her ear. After doing this, remind her how attractive she looks.**

Nothing is more precious or delicate than a flower. In the marriage, let nothing be more precious than your wife. Treat her as if she is your delicate flower.

I am the rose of Sharon, and the lily of the valleys. Song of Solomon 2:1

Results: _____

_____

_____

_____

_____

_____

_____

7) Take notice of the various colors of nail polish that your wife uses and offer to paint her finger and toenails. If she prefers no color, polish them with a coat of clear.

One thing that frustrates most women is that we, as men, are not very observant. Take the time to study your wife. Become familiar with her likes and dislikes.

Likewise, ye husbands, dwell with them according to knowledge, giving honor unto the wife, as unto the weaker vessel, and as being heirs together of the grace of life; that your prayers be not hindered. I Peter 3:7

Results: _____

_____

_____

_____

_____

_____

_____

8)   Wake up early and make breakfast for your wife.

It would probably make her day to have a hot meal when she wakes up in the morning. Remember, you're not the only one who gets hungry. Don't worry if your cooking skills are not the best, she probably doesn't expect for you to be the "Iron Chef".

༄༄༄

Let a little water, I pray you, be fetched, and wash your feet, and rest yourselves under the tree: And I will fetch a morsel of bread, and comfort ye your hearts; after that ye shall pass on: for therefore are ye come to your servant. And they said, so do, as thou hast said. And Abraham hastened into the tent unto Sarah, and said, Make ready quickly three measures of fine meal, knead it, and make cakes upon the hearth. And Abraham ran unto the herd and fetcht a calf tender and good, and gave it unto a young man; and he hasted to dress it. And he took butter, and milk, and the calf which he had dressed, and set it before them; and he stood by them under the tree, and they did eat. Genesis 18:4-8

Results: _____

_____

_____

_____

_____

_____

_____

9)   Prepare your wife a lunch for work.

The little things are sometimes the big things. Kindness is a rare character trait these days. Your consideration will cause her to think pleasantly about you for the remainder of the day.

Put on therefore, as the elect of God, holy and beloved, bowels of mercies, kindness, humbleness of mind, meekness, longsuffering.
Colossians 3:12

Results: _____

_____

_____

_____

_____

_____

_____

10) **Ask her what she would like for dinner, and then prepare it for her.**

Taking the time to prepare your wife a meal is one thing, but when you go out of your way to prepare her favorite dish, that's something totally different. Although she may not verbalize it, she recognizes the sacrifice and the time you put in to make her happy. Keep it up.

And let us not be weary in well doing: for in due season we shall reap, if we faint not. Galatians 6:9

Results: _____

_____

_____

_____

_____

_____

_____

11) **Purchase her favorite magazines and spread them out on the bed. When she gets home, tell her that you'll take care of dinner and the kids while she takes some time to relax.**

Your wife works hard just being your wife, so anytime you can, take some of the load off of her. This way, she will be able to get some needed rest and relaxation. This time will not only benefit her, but you as well.

Give her of the fruit of her hands; and let her own works praise her in the gates. Proverbs 31:31

Results: _____

_____

_____

_____

_____

_____

_____

12)   Hold hands as the two of you fall asleep.

Romance never sleeps, and neither should your pursuit of your wife.

Fear thou not; for I am with thee: be not dismayed; for I am thy God: I will strengthen thee; yea, I will help thee; yea I will uphold thee with the right hand of my righteousness. Isaiah 41:10

Results: _____

_____

_____

_____

_____

_____

_____

13) Tell her all you want to do is hold her as the two of you fall asleep.

Believe it or not guys, sometimes your wife just wants to be held. Show her that you want all of her, and not just her body.

Let thy fountain be blessed: and rejoice with the wife of thy youth. ***Proverbs 5:18***

Results: _____

_____

_____

_____

_____

_____

_____

14)   Hold hands everywhere you go.

God created man, but He took the woman out of what He created. Your wife is a part of you, and because of this, she needs to feel your touch. It is as if the two of you are magnets designed to be together. Holding her hand means more to her than you know.

And the LORD God caused a deep sleep to fall upon Adam, and he slept: and he took one of his ribs, and closed up the flesh instead thereof;

And the rib, which the LORD God had taken from man, made He a woman, and brought her unto the man. Genesis 2:21-22

Results: _____

_____

_____

_____

_____

_____

_____

15) While in public, whisper in your wife's ear that she is the most beautiful woman in the room.

There are not too many women that don't like to hear how beautiful they are, especially coming from their mates. Your wife needs to know that you think she has it going on, and she longs to hear you tell her.

Behold, thou art fair, my love; behold, thou art fair; thou hast doves' eyes. Song of Solomon 1:15

Results: _____

_____

_____

_____

_____

_____

_____

16) Take your wife into your arms and look into her eyes, and just smile.

There is no issue so big that a smile can't cure, especially when you're holding a good-looking woman at the same time.

His left hand is under my head, and his right hand doth embrace me.
Song of Solomon 2:6

Results: _____

_____

_____

_____

_____

_____

_____

17)   Softly kiss her every night before you go to bed, and again
      when you wake up in the morning.

Do you remember the first time you kissed your wife? Allow her to
enjoy that memory every day.

᪥᪥᪥

*Let him kiss me with the kisses of his mouth: for thy love is better
than wine. Song of Solomon 1:2*

Results: _____

_____

_____

_____

_____

_____

_____

18) **Never allow your wife to open a door for herself, never.**

Chivalry never goes out of style. Be a gentleman by always treating your wife like royalty.

For a day in thy courts is better than a thousand. I had rather be a doorkeeper in the house of my God, than to dwell in the tents of wickedness. Psalm 84:10

Results: _____

_____

_____

_____

_____

_____

_____

19)   Write her a handwritten love letter.

God's word is His love letter to the world. If He can take the time to let His creation know how He feels about them, surely you can do the same for your wife.

And thou shalt write them upon the posts of thy house, and on thy gates. Deuteronomy 6:9

Results: _____

_____

_____

_____

_____

_____

_____

20)   Tell her you would marry her all over again.

Visualize in your mind the look on your wife's face the day you asked her to marry you. Do you remember how happy she looked? Why not bring some joy to her life by reconfirming it again?

Come with me from Lebanon, my spouse, with me from Lebanon: look from the top of Amana, from the top of Shenir and Hermon, from the lions' dens, from the mountains of the leopards. Song of Solomon 4:8

Results: _____

_____

_____

_____

_____

_____

_____

21)   Caress her face with your hand while looking into her eyes.

When you first married your wife, you couldn't keep your eyes or hands off of her. Don't stop now.

Not as though I had already attained, either were already perfect: but I follow after, if that I may apprehend that for which also I am apprehended of Christ Jesus. Philippians 3:12

Results: _____

_____

_____

_____

_____

_____

_____

22)   Ask your wife if she's married.

The season that your wife spent as a single woman was probably a tough one with all of the characters that approached her. The very fact that she said yes to you is proof that you were not the norm. Give her a chance to relive the moment.

To everything there is a season, and a time to every purpose under the heaven. Ecclesiastes 3:1

Results: _____

_____

_____

_____

_____

_____

_____

23) When out at a restaurant, make a point to sit on the same side of the table.

Nothing will make you feel more like a teenager than doing things that a teenager would do. You may look foolish to the world, but to your wife, you'll be Prince Charming.

I am my beloved's, and his desire is towards me. Song of Solomon 7:10

Results: _____

_____

_____

_____

_____

_____

_____

24) **Purchase a greeting card, write a love message in it and mail it to your home, addressed to her.**

Everyone likes receiving mail, especially when it's not associated with a bill. Think of the excitement your wife will feel when she opens a card from you containing your deepest thoughts. Nothing could be sweeter.

But this shall be the covenant that I will make with the house of Israel; After those days, saith the LORD, I will put my law in their inward parts, and write it in their hearts; and will be their God, and they shall be my people. Jeremiah 31:33

Results: _____

_____

_____

_____

_____

_____

_____

25)   Stop by your wife's job to just say hello.

If you've been practicing the preceding ideas on romancing your wife, chances are she talks about you frequently at work. What greater way is there for her to show off her man to her friends than when he stops by to say hello.

The light of the eyes rejoiceth the heart: and a good report maketh the bones fat. Proverbs 15:30

Results: _____

_____

_____

_____

_____

_____

_____

26)   Go on a picnic to a local park and take a blanket.

Nothing is more relaxing than eating outside on a beautiful day with a beautiful woman. Spending time like this together is never time wasted.

♪♪♪

Come, my beloved, let us go forth into the field; let us lodge in the villages. Song of Solomon 7:11

Results: _____

_____

_____

_____

_____

_____

_____

27)   Watch one of her favorite movies together.

Okay guys, I know you want to watch the game, but why not give of yourself by watching something that your wife likes for a change. When you make a habit of giving yourself, you're giving your best. Your wife will appreciate you for it.

Fear not: for I am with thee...Isaiah 43:5

Results: _____

_____

_____

_____

_____

_____

28)   Take your wife dancing.

In order to get something out of your marriage that you've never experienced, you're going to have to do something that you've never done before.

Now when he had left speaking, he said unto Simon, Launch out into the deep, and let down your nets for a draught. Luke 5:4

Results: _____

_____

_____

_____

_____

_____

_____

29)   Go roller blading together.

What can I say guys? What else could you do together where you'll actually have fun falling down? The good part is you get to hold her each time you pick her up.

For I the LORD thy God will hold thy right hand, saying unto thee, Fear not; I will help thee. Isaiah 41:13

Results: _____

_____

_____

_____

_____

_____

_____

30)   Leave work early and go home and clean up before she gets there.

There's nothing like coming home to a clean house, especially when you're not the one who has to clean it. Your wife will love you for days after coming home to find that you've taken the time to do this for her. Just think, if she doesn't have to do anything when she gets home, this leaves her with more time to spend with you.

Husbands, love your wives, even as Christ also loved the church, and gave himself for it; Ephesians 5:25

Results: _____

_____

_____

_____

_____

_____

_____

31)   Get dressed up and go to a nice restaurant and share a dessert.

Remember when you were in high school and you didn't have enough money to pay for dinner, but dessert was no problem? Well, let this remind you of that. There's nothing better than sharing sweets with your sweetie.

How sweet are thy words unto my taste! yea, sweeter than honey to my mouth! Psalm 119:103

Results: _____

_____

_____

_____

_____

_____

_____

32)   Go on a carriage ride together.

Men, by all means, treat your wife to an occasional carriage ride. She will feel like Cinderella as the two of you hold each other close.

For thy Maker is thine husband; the LORD of hosts is his name; and thy Redeemer the Holy One of Israel; The God of the whole earth shall he be called. Isaiah 54:5

Results: _____

_____

_____

_____

_____

_____

33) Send your wife on a vacation by herself to her favorite destination.

Men, here is your chance to earn brownie points for the next ten years! Your wife will celebrate your love for her. She will come back relaxed with nothing but you on her mind. Don't be surprised if she brings you back a souvenir!

Nor height, nor depth, nor any other creature, shall be able to separate us from the love of God, which is in Christ Jesus our Lord. Romans 8:39

Results: _____

_____

_____

_____

_____

_____

34)   Always have a camera with you and take lots of pictures together.

Your wife is not only your spouse, she's also your friend. There is something special in spending time with your best friend and chronicling your life together.

A man that hath friends must shew himself friendly: and there is a friend that sticketh closer than a brother. Proverbs 18:24

Results: _____

_____

_____

_____

_____

_____

_____

35)   Take a cooking class together at a local community college.

Everyone loves food, right? This will give the two of you time to bond as you do something that can immediately benefit the both of you. Afterwards, you two could go home and prepare a romantic dinner using the recipes you learned.

Through wisdom is an house builded; and by understanding it is established: Proverbs 24:3

Results: _____

_____

_____

_____

_____

_____

_____

**36)   Have a suitcase packed for the both of you and take an un-
planned three-day weekend.**

Men, if you can take the time and plan a trip to your favorite sporting
event, surely you can plan some time to spend with your wife. Never
underestimate the time you two spend alone, especially when it's a
surprise. Your wife longs to be with her man, so why not give her the
opportunity?

*My beloved spake, and said unto me, Rise up, my love, my fair one,
and come away. Song of Solomon 2:10*

Results: _____

_____

_____

_____

_____

_____

_____

37) **Take a day off of work to nurse your wife back to health whenever she's sick.**

Never go to work and leave your wife home alone when she's sick. Even if she sleeps all day and never notices you, your presence alone is priceless.

But a certain Samaritan, as he journeyed, came where he was: and when he saw him, he had compassion on him, And went to him, and bound up his wounds, pouring in oil and wine, and set him on his own beast, and brought him to an inn, and took care of him. Luke 10:33-34

Results: _____

_____

_____

_____

_____

_____

_____

38)   Always make sure her car has a full tank of gas.

With gas prices going up every day, your wife will really appreciate you taking the time to see that her tank is full. You may even have a surprise waiting for you when you get home!

Then Joseph commanded to fill their sacks with corn, and to restore every man's money into his sack, and to give them provision for the way: and thus did he unto them. Genesis 42:25

Results: _____

_____

_____

_____

_____

_____

_____

39) **Tell her how beautiful she is, and thank her for choosing to marry you.**

There's a reason you asked your wife to marry you. Think about it, she could have married anyone but she said yes to you. Lavish her with praise.

Favour is deceitful, and beauty is vain: but a woman that feareth the LORD, she shall be praised. Proverbs 31:30

Results: _____

_____

_____

_____

_____

_____

_____

**40)   The next time your wife mentions that she's going to wash her
hair, volunteer to do it for her.**

Did I mention that water was involved here? Dim the lights and you've
got yourself an evening to remember.

*Let the husband render unto the wife due benevolence: and likewise
also the wife unto the husband. I Corinthians 7:3*

Results: _____

_____

_____

_____

_____

_____

_____

41) **Book her a hotel room for the weekend so that she can rest while you take care of all the household chores.**

There are many challenges that your wife faces on a daily basis. She probably doesn't share them all with you. A little rest and relaxation is good for everyone, especially for the woman you love.

He maketh me to lie down in green pastures: he leadeth me beside the still waters. Psalm 23:2

Results: _____

_____

_____

_____

_____

_____

_____

42)   The next time the two of you are in public, if you notice her shoe is untied, tie it for her.

I know this may seem childish, and to the world you might even look stupid, but trust me, the one who really matters will love you dearly.

For do I now persuade men, or God? or do I seek to please men? for if I yet pleased men, I should not be the servant of Christ. Galatians 1:10

Results: _____

_____

_____

_____

_____

_____

_____

43)   Pray with her every night before you go to bed.

Anytime you include God in the equation, you can never go wrong. Cover your wife with your prayers daily, and watch God take your relationship to a new dimension.

Two are better than one; because they have a good reward for their labor. For if they fall, the one will lift up his fellow: but woe to him that is alone when he falleth; for he hath not another to help him up. Again, if two lie together, then they have heat: but how can one be warm alone?

And if one prevail against him, two shall withstand him; and a three-fold cord is not quickly broken. Ecclesiastes 4:9-12

Results: _____

_____

_____

_____

_____

_____

_____

44)   **Take her to the place where the two of you first met, and re-enact the moment.**

The very fact that you remember where you met your wife will put a smile on her face. Reenact the moment and she'll be like putty in your hands.

And the LORD said, Behold, there is a place by me, and thou shalt stand upon a rock: Exodus 33:21

Results: _____

_____

_____

_____

_____

_____

45)   Go to the park and spend hours talking about your dreams for the future.

Spending time at a ball game is certainly more appealing to most men than just browsing around the park, but believe me, it will be well worth the investment of your time.

Live joyfully with the wife whom thou lovest all the days of the life of thy vanity, which he hath given thee under the sun, all the days of thy vanity: for that is thy portion in this life, and in thy labour which thou takest under the sun. Ecclesiastes 9:9

Results: _____

_____

_____

_____

_____

_____

_____

46)	**If you don't have the money to take her on a dream vacation, plan several mini vacations that will require the two of you spending hours in the car talking.**

Studies show that women talk three times more during the day than men. Give her the chance to reveal her heart to you while the two of you go some place special.

Incline your ear, and come unto me: hear, and your soul shall live; and I will make an everlasting covenant with you, even the sure mercies of David. Isaiah 55:3

Results: _____

_____

_____

_____

_____

_____

_____

47) Take her to a jazz club where the two of you can listen to music.

We've all seen movies with couples sitting in some nice jazz club with the lights dimmed, drinking a glass of wine. Even if your wife is not a big fan of jazz music, the atmosphere will reignite what was lost through the busyness of life.

And it came to pass, when the evil spirit from God was upon Saul, that David took an harp, and played with his hand: so Saul was refreshed, and was well, and the evil spirit departed from him. I Samuel 16:23

Results: _____

_____

_____

_____

_____

_____

_____

48) Have your bedroom painted in her favorite color while she is away at work.

Women like men who are creative, men who think outside the box. She'll be totally surprised when she returns home to find that her personal sanctuary has been transformed.

And God said, Let the earth bring forth grass, the herb yielding seed, and the fruit tree yielding fruit after his kind, whose seed is in itself, upon the earth: and it was so. And the earth brought forth grass and herb yielding seed after his kind, and the tree yielding fruit, whose seed was in itself, after his kind: and God saw that it was good. Genesis 1:11-12

Results: _____

_____

_____

_____

_____

_____

_____

49) Buy a book of poetry and read her a poem every night before bed.

Imagine the two of you cuddled up next to each other while you read your wife a poem. Now imagine that after you finish reading, the two of you decide to stay up a little later than you originally planned.

Wherefore his servants said unto him, Let there be sought for my lord the king a young virgin: and let her stand before the king, and let her cherish him, and let her lie in thy bosom, that my lord the king may get heat. I Kings 1:2

Results: _____

_____

_____

_____

_____

_____

_____

50) **When you have to make a decision on whether to work late or go home to spend time with your wife, choose your wife, always!**

Many marriages have ended because men forgot that their first responsibility was to their family, not their employer. Don't allow your job to be the other woman in your life.

Nevertheless I have somewhat against thee, because thou hast left thy first love. Revelation 2:4

Results: _____

_____

_____

_____

_____

_____

_____

51) **Ask God to reveal to you your wife's desires and the means to meet them.**

There are some things that you don't know about your wife. God, on the other hand, knows every little detail about her. Allow Him to reveal to you the things that will bring a smile to her face.

The eyes of your understanding being enlightened; that ye may know what is the hope of his calling, and what the riches of the glory of his inheritance in the saints. Ephesians 1:18

Results: _____

_____

_____

_____

_____

_____

_____

52) **Have pictures of the two of you framed, and present the picture to her as a gift.**

They say that a picture is worth a thousand words. Placing pictures of the two of you around your home will help you during the dry seasons of your marriage.

But we all, with open face beholding as in a glass the glory of the Lord, are changed into the same image from glory to glory, even as by the Spirit of the Lord. II Corinthians 3:18

Results: _____

_____

_____

_____

_____

_____

_____

53)   Purchase her three most favorite perfumes and have them professionally wrapped for her.

It doesn't always have to be a holiday or special occasion for you to give your wife a gift. Whenever she uses her new perfume, you will know that she was present, even if she's not in the room. She will remember you for it.

✷✷✷

And when they were come into the house, they saw the young child with Mary his mother, and fell down, and worshipped him: and when they had opened their treasures, they presented unto him gifts; gold, and frankincense and myrrh. Matthew 2:11

Results: _____

_____

_____

_____

_____

_____

_____

54)   Take the time to load her MP3 player with all of her favorite music.

I know this one may be a chore, but your wife will adore you for thinking of her, especially since she didn't have to pay for the down loaded songs.

But this I say, He which soweth sparingly shall reap also sparingly; and he which soweth bountifully shall reap also bountifully. II Corinthians 9:6

Results: _____

_____

_____

_____

_____

_____

55) Take note of the size that she wears, and buy her an outfit that you think she would like.

Even if your wife doesn't like what you choose, she'll be just as happy because you took the time to think of her.

For God is not unrighteous to forget your work and labour of love, which ye have shewed toward his name, in that ye have ministered to the saints, and do minister. Hebrews 6:10

Results: _____

_____

_____

_____

_____

_____

_____

56) **Take a half-day off work and make a trip to her job just to see how she's doing. Bring flowers and a picnic basket.**

Although she may not verbalize it, your wife would love to see you during the day. Know that you'll be on her mind for the rest of the day.

Get wisdom, get understanding: forget it not; neither decline from the words of my mouth. Forsake her not, and she shall preserve thee: love her, and she shall keep thee. Wisdom is the principal thing; therefore get wisdom: and with all thy getting get understanding. Exalt her, and she shall promote thee: she shall bring thee to honour, when thou dost embrace her. She shall give to thine head an ornament of grace: a crown of glory shall she deliver to thee. Proverbs 4:5-9

Results: _____

_____

_____

_____

_____

_____

_____

57)   Purchase her favorite scented candles.

Guys, if you haven't noticed, most women like things that smell good. Why not purchase some candles to brighten her day?

Ye are the light of the world. A city that is set on a hill cannot be hid.
Matthew 5:14

Results: _____

_____

_____

_____

_____

_____

_____

58)   When you know that she's stressed, and having a bad day, take the time to actively listen without trying to solve the problem.

Your wife doesn't always want your advice. Sometimes, she just wants you to listen.

So that thou incline thine ear unto wisdom, and apply thine heart to understanding; Proverbs 2:2

Results: _____

_____

_____

_____

_____

_____

59)   Make a point to hug her at least three times a day.

It's a proven fact that hugging improves your health. Think about it this way, with every hug, you could be saving money on unnecessary medical bills.

A time to cast away stones, and a time to gather stones together; a time to embrace, and a time to refrain from embracing; Ecclesiastes 3:5

Results: _____

_____

_____

_____

_____

_____

_____

60)   Kiss her hand while in public.

Your wife desires for you to be her Romeo. The world desperately needs to see true love between a husband and his wife. Give them something to look at in the two of you.

And Jacob kissed Rachel, and lifted up his voice, and wept. Genesis 29:11

Results: _____

_____

_____

_____

_____

_____

_____

61)   Spend a Sunday afternoon relaxing while eating ice cream together.

Sunday afternoons are so relaxing. Why not wind down with some good ice cream. If she asks to taste yours, purposely get some on her nose so you can lick it off.

And God blessed the seventh day, and sanctified it: because that in it he had rested from all his work which God created and made. Genesis 2:3

Results: _____

_____

_____

_____

_____

_____

_____

62) **Purchase bicycles. Make a habit of going for bike rides in the park.**

Being married doesn't have to be boring. Have some fun with the woman you love.

Let Israel rejoice in him that made him: let the children of Zion be joyful in their King. Let them praise his name in the dance: let them sing praises unto him with the timbrel and harp. Psalm 149:2-3

Results: _____

_____

_____

_____

_____

_____

_____

63)   When your funds are low, have a candle light pizza dinner.

Chances are your wife didn't marry you for your money, she married you because she loved you. Therefore, don't think that you have to spend lots of money at fancy restaurants to show her that you love her. Who knows, she may even allow you to have the last slice.

Not that I speak in respect of want: for I have learned, in whatsoever state I am, therewith to be content. I know both how to be abased, and I know how to abound: everywhere and in all things I am instructed both to be full and to be hungry, both to abound and to suffer need. I can do all things through Christ which strengtheneth me. Philippians 4:11-13

Results: _____

_____

_____

_____

_____

_____

_____

64) Tell her you love her over and over and over again, saying her name each time.

Although she may know it, your wife needs to hear you say that you love her, and what's more sensual than saying I love you continually to the most beautiful woman you've ever laid eyes on?

Stay me with flagons, comfort me with apples: for I am sick of love.
Song of Solomon 2:5

Results: _____

_____

_____

_____

_____

_____

_____

65) Leave work early and have the house setup with candles lit, dinner prepared, and Luther Vandross, or some other soft music playing in the background. Don't forget to ask her about her day.

If the sound of Luther's voice or some other soft music doesn't make your wife melt in your hands, then if I were you, I would check her pulse to see if she's breathing.

And my people shall dwell in a peaceable habitation, and in sure dwellings, and in quiet resting places: Isaiah 32:18

Results: _____

_____

_____

_____

_____

_____

_____

66)   Spend a Saturday afternoon helping her clean out her closet.

If your wife is like most women, she has lots of clothes. Most of them, she probably doesn't even wear. You will probably relieve a big load by helping bring some order to her closet, but beware, this may be an incentive for her to go out and buy more stuff, stuff that you'll probably have to pay for.

Two are better than one; because they have a good reward for their labour. Ecclesiastes 4:9

Results: _____

_____

_____

_____

_____

_____

_____

67) Take her to a movie, and while the previews are showing, spend that time kissing.

If this doesn't bring back memories of your high school days, I don't know what will. The ten minutes you spend being intimate will be well worth the price of admission.

And it came to pass, when he had been there a long time, that Abimelech king of the Philistines looked out at a window, and saw, and, behold, Isaac was sporting with Rebekah his wife. Genesis 26:8

Results: _____

_____

_____

_____

_____

_____

_____

68)   After dinner, go for a long walk.

I often hear a lot of women say they wish they could lose some weight. Well, what better way to lose a few pounds and bond with the one you love at the same time?

❧❧❧

And they heard the voice of the LORD God walking in the garden in the cool of the day: and Adam and his wife hid themselves from the presence of the LORD God amongst the trees of the garden. Genesis 3:8

Results: _____

_____

_____

_____

_____

_____

69) Hire a cleaning service to help keep the house clean so that the two of you will have more free time to spend together.

As long as you live, there will always be some house cleaning to do. Surprisingly, hiring a cleaning service is not very expensive at all. It will be well worth the money you spend.

Be still, and know that I am God: I will be exalted among the heathen, I will be exalted in the earth. Psalm 46:10

Results: _____

_____

_____

_____

_____

_____

_____

70)   While your wife is away from home, clean her bathroom for her.

Your wife's bathroom is probably the only place in your house where she can get some peace and quiet, so, it would make sense to have it nice and clean when she gets home. Try placing some of the scented candles that I previously mentioned all around the tub, thus creating her private oasis.

And by knowledge shall the chambers be filled with all precious and pleasant riches. Proverbs 24:4

Results: _____

_____

_____

_____

_____

_____

_____

71) **Purchase new bedding. Place fresh flowers in a vase by your bedside.**

Imagine you're in a vast meadow with a sea of colorful flowers all around you. That's the same type of atmosphere you want to create in your bedroom. Trust me when I say that you can never go wrong with fresh flowers.

And why take ye thought for raiment? Consider the lilies of the field, how they grow; they toil not, neither do they spin: And yet I say unto you, that even Solomon in all his glory was not arrayed like one of these. Mattthew 6:28-29

Results: _____

_____

_____

_____

_____

_____

_____

72) **Purposely park near the back of the parking lot at the grocery store so the two of you can hold hands while taking the long walk to the entrance.**

This may seem silly, and not to mention, inconvenient, but the goal is to increase your quality time together. Remember, the deposits of kindness, thoughtfulness, and compassion that you make in your relationship today will cause you to reap great rewards in the future.

Give, and it shall be given unto you; good measure, pressed down, and shaken together, and running over, shall men give into your bosom. For with the same measure that ye mete withal it shall be measured to you again. Luke 6:38

Results: _____

_____

_____

_____

_____

_____

_____

73) **Ask her to go in the store while you stay in the car. Tell her the reason you want to stay is so you can watch her as she walks away.**

Your wife wants to know that you think she's sexy. She understands that there are many women out there that can divert your attention and for you to choose to look at her in that way will make her feel good.

And it came to pass in an evening tide, that David arose from off his bed, and walked upon the roof of the king's house: and from the roof he saw a woman washing herself; and the woman was very beautiful to look upon. II Samuel 11:2

Results: _____

_____

_____

_____

_____

_____

74) **Hang some mistletoe over your bedroom door during the summer months, and every time you enter the room, kiss her as if it were going to be the last time you will ever see her.**

Men, the goal is to be creative, and you'll score big with this one. You may find that your wife will be waiting for you at the threshold of your bedroom door every time the two of you are home. Good luck if you ever try to suggest taking the mistletoe down.

And he went down, and talked with the woman; and she pleased Samson well. Judges 14:7

Results: _____

_____

_____

_____

_____

_____

75) If you have children, hire a babysitter at least once a week as the two of you go off and recharge on a long drive. Tell her that she's even more beautiful than when you first met her.

Anytime the two of you can break away from the kids and spend some quality time together, your marriage will be made better. Many couples tend to put their relationship on the back burner once children come on the scene, but if you neglect your marriage then the children will suffer in the end. After God, always put your wife first. Always!

And Pharaoh's daughter said unto her, Take this child away, and nurse it for me, and I will give thee thy wages. And the women took the child, and nursed it. Exodus 2:9

Results: _____

_____

_____

_____

_____

_____

_____

76)   Go to the park and feed the ducks.

Nature has a way of bringing out the best in everyone. This idea will help the two of you to reconnect, relax, and smile more. These things are important in every marriage.

Behold the fowls of the air: for they sow not, neither do they reap, nor gather into barns; yet your heavenly Father feedeth them. Are ye not much better than they? Matthew 6:26

Results: _____

_____

_____

_____

_____

_____

77)   Spend a day outside planting flowers together.

Although this will require work, think of it this way: your lawn will benefit and afterwards the two of you will look all shiny and sweaty which may not be a bad idea.

The LORD hath appeared of old unto me, saying, Yea, I have loved thee with an everlasting love: therefore with loving-kindness have I drawn thee. Again I will build thee, and thou shalt be built, O virgin of Israel: thou shalt again be adorned with thy tabrets, and shalt go forth in the dances of them that make merry. Thou shalt yet plant vines upon the mountains of Samaria: the planters shall plant, and shall eat them as common things. Jeremiah 31:3-5

Results: _____

_____

_____

_____

_____

_____

78)   Wake up early each Saturday morning and go get fresh flowers for the breakfast table.

As mentioned previously, you can never go wrong with fresh flowers. There's nothing better than sitting down to a hot meal with the one you love. Adding flowers to the mix just makes the day that much better.

And he shall be like a tree planted by the rivers of water, that bringeth forth his fruit in his season; his leaf also shall not wither; and whatsoever he doeth shall prosper. Psalm 1:3

Results: _____

_____

_____

_____

_____

_____

79) **Get in shape by exercising more so that you can be at your best physically, emotionally, and spiritually.**

Although this idea may not seem very romantic, your health is important, not only to you, but also to your wife. Therefore, be sure to stay fit. Your wife will appreciate your diligence in the years to come.

Behold, I will bring it health and cure, and I will cure them, and will reveal unto them the abundance of peace and truth. And I will cause the captivity of Judah and the captivity of Israel to return, and will build them, as at the first. Jeremiah 33:6-7

Results: _____

_____

_____

_____

_____

_____

80)   Tell her your innermost secrets.

The object here guys is to share things about yourself that will cause your wife to see you differently, in a positive way of course. I'm sure there are several interesting facts about you that your wife never knew. Your revealing them to her will prove that you trust her with your deepest secrets.

And Solomon told her all her questions: and there was nothing hid from Solomon which he told her not. II Chronicles 9:2

Results: _____

_____

_____

_____

_____

_____

81) Take her to a museum or to the theater to watch a live play.

I can imagine what you may be thinking: museums are boring and you would rather watch paint dry than go to a play. What I need you to understand is that it's not about you it's about your wife. You're the one that's trying to improve in the romance department, right? Then, be careful not to think small, and don't be afraid to do something different. Who knows, you just may enjoy yourself.

Remember ye not the former things, neither consider the things of old. Behold, I will do a new thing; now it shall spring forth; shall ye not know it? I will even make a way in the wilderness, and rivers in the desert. Isaiah 43:18-19

Results: _____

_____

_____

_____

_____

_____

_____

82)   Purchase small gifts that are special to her and give her one each day of the week.

Gifts don't have to cost a fortune. Set a budget of $50 and purchase items that you know she will enjoy. Your wife is your queen and should be treated as such.

A man's gift maketh room for him, and bringeth him before great men. Proverbs 18:16

Results: _____

_____

_____

_____

_____

_____

_____

83)   Have a warm bubble bath waiting for her when she gets home.

Your wife has probably had a rough day working with people who neither appreciate nor value her presence. Show her how much she means to you by having a hot bath prepared.

Now when every maid's turn was come to go in to king Ahasuerus, after that she had been twelve months, according to the manner of the women, for so were the days of their purifications accomplished, to wit, six months with oil of myrrh, and six months with sweet odors, and with other things for the purifying of the women; Esther 2:12

Results: _____

_____

_____

_____

_____

_____

_____

84) Purchase a book on names and write her a note with the meaning of her name. You could even look it up online.

There is a lot in a person's name. Many people never take the time to research what their name means. For you to do this will show her that you have the ability to think outside of the box.

Then they that feared the LORD spake often one to another: and the LORD hearkened, and heard it, and a book of remembrance was written before him for them that feared the LORD, and that thought upon his name. Malachi 3:16

Results: _____

_____

_____

_____

_____

_____

_____

85) **Spend a day at an amusement park having fun.**

Who doesn't like an amusement park? Lighten up and have some fun with the woman you love. Doing more things together will add more spice to your life.

There is nothing better for a man, than that he should eat and drink, and that he should make his soul enjoy good in his labour. This also I saw, that it was from the hand of God. Ecclesiastes 2:24

Results: _____

_____

_____

_____

_____

_____

_____

86)   Go to a bakery and have her favorite cake made. Top the cake with the words, "Just because I love you".

You don't have to have a reason to be good to your wife. Being good to her should come natural. Keep her on her toes by making her feel special when she least expects it.

And now abideth faith, hope, charity, these three; but the greatest of these is charity. I Corinthians 13:13

Results: _____

_____

_____

_____

_____

_____

_____

87)   Book a room at the most expensive hotel in your city, spare no expense. Have her bag already packed without her knowledge and when she gets home Friday evening, tell her this weekend the two of you will reconnect.

Women love surprises. It will truly surprise her when she finds out that she'll be able to spend some quality time alone with her man.

Then shall the kingdom of heaven be likened unto ten virgins, which took their lamps, and went forth to meet the bridegroom. Matthew 25:1

Results: _____

_____

_____

_____

_____

_____

_____

88) Make a point to touch her in a non-sexual way every time she enters the room.

Now guys, I know that your wife is irresistible, but this will require some self control on your part. The goal is to gently caress your wife, not grope her. Despite what you think, she doesn't always feel up to being intimate. Besides, there's more to a marriage than sex.

I charge you, O ye daughters of Jerusalem, by the roes, and by the hinds of the field, that ye stir not up, nor awake my love, till he please. Song of Solomon 2:7

Results: _____

_____

_____

_____

_____

_____

89)   Sacrifice to save as much money as you can throughout the year so that you can surprise her with a shopping spree.

Your wife can always use more clothes, right? Even if you think she has too much already, let her have a day where she can splurge on herself and not feel guilty.

Beloved, I wish above all things that thou mayest prosper and be in health, even as thy soul prospereth. III John 1:2

Results: _____

_____

_____

_____

_____

_____

_____

90) **While at a party, or at a friend's house, ask her to come in the other room while the two of you sneak in a few kisses.**

Come on now guys, you know this sounds fun. Who cares if someone catches the two of you smooching in the next room? Your wife is well worth the embarrassment.

Defraud ye not one the other, except it be with consent for a time, that ye may give yourselves to fasting and prayer; and come together again, that Satan tempt you not for your incontinency. I Corinthians 7:5

Results: _____

_____

_____

_____

_____

_____

_____

91)   Tell her how beautiful she is in public around others.

Never let an opportunity go by where you don't communicate your love for your wife. Your wife is the gift that God has given you. Honor her as such.

I will praise thee; for I am fearfully and wonderfully made: marvelous are thy works; and that my soul knoweth right well. Psalm 139:14

Results: _____

_____

_____

_____

_____

_____

_____

92) When traveling on an airplane, ask the stewardess if the pilot could announce your wife's name over the intercom. Make sure they address her as the most attractive woman on the flight.

She may be embarrassed during the flight, but believe me, she'll hold your hand the whole time. Let the world know how blessed you are to have her in your life.

And the men of the place asked him of his wife; and he said, She is my sister: for he feared to say, She is my wife; lest, said he, the men of the place should kill me for Rebekah; because she was fair to look upon. Genesis 26:7

Results: _____

_____

_____

_____

_____

_____

_____

93) **Instead of celebrating Thanksgiving or Christmas the traditional way, stay at a bed and breakfast, pampering her the whole time.**

Go off and celebrate the holidays together. This will be a time the two of you will never forget. Your family will understand if you miss one gathering.

❧❧❧❧

Three times thou shalt keep a feast unto me in the year. Exodus 23:14

Results: _____

_____

_____

_____

_____

_____

_____

94) **Ask your wife's parents to give you pictures of her when she was a child. Put them together in a slideshow. Invite friends over for dinner, in celebration of your wife, and when everyone sits down to have dessert, play the slideshow, to her surprise.**

Your wife is the star attraction in your life and should be treated that way. Instead of always taunting your accomplishments, promote your wife and you'll be richly rewarded.

Many daughters have done virtuously, but thou excellest them all. Proverbs 31:29

Results: _____

_____

_____

_____

_____

_____

95)   While in public, pass your wife a hand written note telling her how sexy she looks.

Now here's a scandalous but adventuresome idea. Pursue your wife as if she were someone you wanted to marry, and watch the sparks fly.

Leah was tender eyed; but Rachel was beautiful and well favored.
Genesis 29:17

Results: _____

_____

_____

_____

_____

_____

_____

96) **For thirty days, before coming home, stop at a florist and purchase a single rose to give to her. Be careful not to skip a day.**

Consistency is the key! Week one she'll think you're trying to butter her up. Week two she'll be wondering what's come over you. Week three she'll go to work every day with a smile on her face. When week four comes along, anything that you may have done to upset her will be a distant memory.

That he might present it to himself a glorious church, not having spot, or wrinkle, or any such thing; but that it should be holy and without blemish. Ephesians 5:27

Results: _____

_____

_____

_____

_____

_____

_____

97)   Tell her how you feel about her in front of her family.

Guys do this one time and you'll be on your in-laws good side forever. You will earn your wife's devotion at the same time.

And she spake out with a loud voice, and said, Blessed art thou among women, and blessed is the fruit of thy womb. Luke 1:42

Results: _____

_____

_____

_____

_____

_____

_____

98) **Walk up behind her and kiss her on the back of the neck while whispering something sweet in her ear. Doing this in public will earn you extra brownie points.**

Key words here are kiss, neck, and whisper. Need I say more?

Who can find a virtuous woman? For her price is far above rubies. Proverbs 31:10

Results: _____

_____

_____

_____

_____

_____

_____

99)   Prepay her hairstylist for 10 visits so that she never has to come out of pocket to get her hair done.

Is there any woman who doesn't like to get her hair done? Throwing in a free hair-do makes one happy woman!

And on the morrow when he departed, he took out two pence, and gave them to the host, and said unto him, Take care of him; and whatsoever thou spendest more, when I come again, I will repay thee. Luke 10:35

Results: _____

_____

_____

_____

_____

_____

_____

100) Schedule a weekly appointment to get her nails done.

Your wife is a reflection of you. When she looks good, you look good!

♪♪♪

So ought men to love their wives as their own bodies. He that loveth his wife loveth himself. Ephesians 5:28

Results: _____

_____

_____

_____

_____

_____

_____

101) Offer to pick her up at work, and arrive 20 minutes early. Spend this time telling all of her co-workers how blessed you are to have her in your life.

Praise, praise, praise; what woman do you know that doesn't like to be praised, especially when she's your wife? By doing this, every woman that works in her office will wonder what your wife is doing to earn such admiration.

Whoso findeth a wife findeth a good thing, and obtaineth favour of the LORD. Proverbs 18:22

Results: _____

_____

_____

_____

_____

_____

_____

Epilogue

The purpose of this book was to encourage husbands to continually pursue their wives, just as they did when they first met. A wife is a gift from God, and it pleases Him when we show appreciation for the things that He gives us.

Not all of my suggestions will work for the woman that is in your life, which is why I expressed the importance of intimately knowing your wife. It is pertinent that you be well aware of her likes and dislikes. The ones that work best for you are the ones that I suggest you often use.

These admonitions need not be practiced every day, but the more you practice them, the more you are sure to rekindle the flames that burned in the heat of your marriage to your precious wife.

In addition to writing, Charles Roberts enjoys a ministry of public speaking. If you would like more information, please contact: Clroberts33@gmail.com or visit www.charlesrobertsonline.com

CPSIA information can be obtained at www.ICGtesting.com
Printed in the USA
LVOW10s0753050715

444993LV00001B/1/P

9 781432 778187